Mastery in Motion

Strategies for Influence and Triumph

Foreword

In the ceaseless journey toward personal and professional success, we traverse landscapes fraught with challenges and opportunities, weaving through the intricate tapestry of human interaction and ambition. "Mastery in Motion: Strategies for Influence and Triumph" by Michael Jensen serves as a guiding beacon through these dynamic terrains.

This book is not a mere collection of theories; it is a culmination of distilled wisdom from centuries of strategic thinking, tempered by the fires of experience and adaptation.

Its aim is singular: to equip you with the tools and insights necessary to navigate the complex interplay of power, influence, and achievement.

Within these pages lie the blueprints of strategic brilliance, drawn not from the corridors of power or the battlegrounds of conquest alone but from the subtle nuances of human interaction, negotiation, and mastery. It's an invitation to decode the intricate dance of strategy, revealing the threads that bind influence and triumph.

The journey toward mastery is not a solitary endeavor; it is a collaborative symphony orchestrated by understanding the nuances of power dynamics, the art of negotiation, and the virtuosity of influence. As you delve into these chapters, consider them not as dictums but as guiding stars illuminating your path toward personal mastery.

"Mastery in Motion" is an odyssey that unfolds within your mind, inviting introspection, action, and evolution. It is a testament to the timeless nature of strategic brilliance and a reminder that the pursuit of influence and triumph is as much an art as it is a science.

May these words serve as your compass, guiding you through the ever-shifting tides of opportunity and challenge. Embrace these strategies, adapt them to your unique journey, and chart a course toward the mastery of influence and triumph.

Let the journey begin.

– Michael Jensen (Author of this brilliant book)

Table of Contents

Conclusion: Charting Your Course of Mastery

Part I: Foundations of Strategic Brilliance

In the tapestry of achievement and influence, strategic brilliance serves as the loom upon which victories are woven. To embark on this journey, one must first lay the groundwork by understanding the foundational elements that constitute strategic brilliance.

The Essence of Strategy

At its core, strategy is the art of envisioning an objective and charting a course to achieve it. It's not just about grand plans but the meticulous alignment of resources, actions, and timing to navigate the ever-shifting landscapes of opportunity and challenge.

Strategic Thinking: A Mental Canvas

Strategic brilliance begins with the cultivation of a mindset—one that sees beyond the immediate horizon and perceives the interconnectedness of actions and consequences. Strategic thinking involves assessing situations holistically, discerning patterns, and anticipating outcomes to make informed decisions.

The Art of Adaptation

Flexibility is the hallmark of strategic brilliance. Rigidity in strategy often leads to stagnation; adaptability, however, enables maneuverability in the face of change. Embracing the fluidity of circumstances and recalibrating strategies accordingly is pivotal for sustained success.

Negotiation as a Strategic Tool

In the arsenal of strategic brilliance lies negotiation—an art form that transcends mere deal-making. Negotiation, when approached strategically, is the gateway to forging alliances, resolving conflicts, and creating mutually beneficial outcomes.

Strategic Vision: Beyond the Immediate

A key attribute of strategic brilliance is the ability to envision not just short-term gains but also long-term objectives.

Cultivating a vision that extends beyond the present moment allows for the alignment of actions with overarching goals.

The Ethics of Strategy

While strategic brilliance empowers individuals, it is underpinned by ethical considerations. The ethical dimension of strategy underscores the importance of integrity, fairness, and moral responsibility in the pursuit and execution of strategic objectives.

Conclusion

Laying the groundwork for strategic brilliance demands a comprehensive understanding of these foundational elements. It is the mastery of these principles that lays the groundwork for navigating the complexities of influence and triumph, setting the stage for a journey toward strategic excellence.

Part II: Navigating the Terrain of Influence

Influence, the invisible force that shapes decisions and propels change, demands a nuanced understanding of the diverse landscapes it traverses. Navigating this multifaceted terrain requires a deliberate exploration of the avenues through which influence manifests and thrives.

Adaptability in Influence

One of the fundamental principles of influence is adaptability—a dynamic capability to adjust strategies according to the context and audience. Understanding that different environments demand varying approaches empowers influencers to resonate with diverse audiences.

Building Credibility and Trust

The bedrock of influential relationships lies in the establishment of credibility and trust. Authenticity, consistency, and competence serve as cornerstones, fostering an environment where influence can flourish organically.

The Power of Networks

Influence extends beyond individual prowess; it flourishes within networks and communities. The adept navigation of social networks and the cultivation of meaningful connections amplify an individual's sphere of influence and facilitate the dissemination of ideas.

Emotional Intelligence: A Key to Influence

Emotional intelligence, the ability to understand and manage emotions, plays a pivotal role in wielding influence. Being attuned to the emotional landscape of interactions enables influencers to connect deeply and resonate with others.

Harnessing the Psychology of Influence

Delving into the intricacies of human psychology unveils the mechanisms that drive influence. Understanding cognitive biases, motivations, and behavioral patterns empowers influencers to craft messages and strategies that resonate effectively.

The Balancing Act: Assertiveness and Empathy

Effective influence entails striking a balance between assertiveness and empathy. While assertiveness conveys confidence and conviction, empathy fosters understanding and rapport—a delicate equilibrium essential for sustained influence.

Conclusion

Mastering the navigation of influence demands a multidimensional approach—one that acknowledges the subtleties of human interaction, psychology, and connectivity. Embracing the complexities of this terrain empowers individuals to wield influence strategically, forging paths toward triumph and impact.

Part III: Tactics for Triumph

Triumph, the culmination of strategic brilliance and influential prowess, is not a mere happenstance but a result of deliberate actions and astute maneuvers. Understanding and employing tactics that catalyze triumph is key to realizing one's objectives in the ever-evolving landscape of achievement.

Strategic Execution: Turning Plans into Reality

Execution excellence is the linchpin upon which triumph rests. Transforming strategic visions into tangible outcomes demands meticulous planning, resource allocation, and the unwavering commitment to see plans through to fruition.

Anticipating and Adapting to Challenges

Triumph is often born from adversity. Recognizing potential obstacles and devising contingency plans is essential for navigating unforeseen challenges. Adaptability in the face of adversity ensures that setbacks become stepping stones toward eventual victory.

The Art of Timing

Timing is a critical factor in the pursuit of triumph. Knowing when to act, when to wait, and when to pivot can make the difference between success and failure. Strategic timing amplifies the impact of actions, maximizing their effectiveness.

Innovative Approaches: Thinking Beyond Conventions

Triumph often emerges from innovative thinking and unconventional approaches. Embracing creativity and challenging traditional paradigms opens doors to new opportunities and solutions that lead to remarkable triumphs.

Risk Management and Calculated Ventures

Triumph requires a calculated approach to risk. Balancing the potential gains against the risks involved and making informed decisions is pivotal. Strategic risk-taking, when calculated and well-managed, can propel one toward unparalleled triumph.

Collaboration and Collective Triumph

Triumph is not solely an individual endeavor; it often emerges from collaborative efforts. Fostering a culture of collaboration and synergy amplifies collective strengths, leading to triumphs that transcend individual achievements.

Conclusion

Tactics for triumph are the strategic maneuvers that transform visions into reality. Embracing these tactics, honing them to match the contours of individual endeavors, and wielding them adeptly is the hallmark of those destined for remarkable triumphs in their pursuits.

Part IV: Mastery Unveiled

Mastery, the pinnacle of relentless dedication and continuous refinement, transcends expertise—it embodies a holistic understanding and application of strategic brilliance, influence, and the art of triumph. Unveiling mastery illuminates the path toward sustained excellence and impact.

Leadership in Motion: The Essence of Mastery

At the heart of mastery lies the essence of leadership—a multifaceted quality that inspires, guides, and empowers. Mastery in leadership is not just about authority but about influence, vision, and the ability to catalyze collective potential toward a shared goal.

Continuous Learning and Adaptation

Mastery is a perpetual journey marked by an insatiable thirst for knowledge and growth. Embracing a mindset of continuous learning and adaptation is fundamental to staying at the forefront of one's field and evolving alongside ever-changing landscapes.

The Art of Mentorship and Contribution

Mastery extends beyond personal achievements; it encompasses the art of mentorship and contribution. Guiding others, sharing insights, and contributing to the growth of individuals and communities perpetuates the cycle of mastery.

Purpose-driven Mastery: Aligning Actions with Values

True mastery is rooted in purpose—a deep alignment of actions with core values and beliefs. When mastery is steered by a profound sense of purpose, accomplishments bear significance beyond individual success, resonating with broader causes and ideals.

Resilience and the Mastery Mindset

Resilience is the bedrock upon which mastery is built. Embracing setbacks as learning opportunities, maintaining focus amid challenges, and bouncing back from failures with renewed determination are hallmarks of the mastery mindset.

Legacy and Impact: Beyond Personal Mastery

The ultimate measure of mastery lies not solely in personal achievements but in the enduring impact left on the world. Crafting a legacy that transcends individual accomplishments, inspiring future generations, and contributing to lasting change define mastery in its most profound sense.

Conclusion

Mastery is not a destination but an ever-evolving journey—one that requires dedication, passion, and a relentless pursuit of excellence. Unveiling mastery involves embodying leadership, embracing continuous learning, and leaving a legacy that resonates through time.

Conclusion: Charting Your Course of Mastery

The journey toward mastery is a tapestry woven with the threads of strategic brilliance, influence, and triumph. As you navigate the ever-evolving landscapes of achievement, consider these guiding principles to chart your course of mastery:

Embrace Strategic Thinking

Cultivate a mindset that transcends the immediate and sees beyond obstacles, envisioning the convergence of actions toward a greater purpose. Strategic thinking serves as the compass that guides your decisions and actions toward mastery.

Hone the Tools of Influence

Delve into the intricacies of influence—understand its nuances, adapt to diverse contexts, and build genuine connections. Mastery of influence empowers you to navigate relationships, negotiate complexities, and effect meaningful change.

Adapt and Innovate

Embrace change as an opportunity for growth. Adaptability and innovation are not just survival skills but catalysts for mastery. Continuously refine your strategies, challenge conventions, and explore new frontiers.

Execute with Precision

Execution excellence is the bridge between strategy and triumph. Ensure that your plans are not just visionary but meticulously executed, leveraging timing, resources, and resilience to turn visions into reality.

Lead with Purpose

Leadership, rooted in purpose and guided by principles, magnifies the impact of mastery. Lead not just by authority but by inspiration, fostering a culture of growth, collaboration, and collective achievement.

Leave a Lasting Legacy

Mastery extends beyond personal accomplishments—it echoes in the lives touched, the knowledge shared, and the legacy crafted. Strive to leave a legacy that transcends time, inspiring others to pursue their paths of mastery.

Continued Pursuit of Mastery

Remember, the pursuit of mastery is an ongoing journey, not a finite destination. Embrace each step, learn from every experience, and remain committed to the relentless pursuit of excellence.

Chart your course with these principles as guiding stars, allowing them to illuminate your path toward mastery—a journey marked not just by achievements but by the profound impact you create along the way.